THE BOOK OF
LAME EXCUSES

ILLUSTRATIONS BY DAN PIRARO

CHRONICLE BOOKS ▪ SAN FRANCISCO

Library of Congress Cataloging-in-Publication Data

The Book of lame excuses / illustrations by Dan Piraro.
    p.   cm.
   ISBN 0-87701-773-5
   1. Excuses—Humor.   I. Piraro, Dan.
   PN6231.E87866   1991   91-12942
   818'.5402—dc20   CIP

Book and cover design: Ann Flanagan Typography, Berkeley, CA
Printed in Hong Kong

Distributed in Canada by Raincoast Books,
112 East Third Avenue, Vancouver, B.C. V5T 1C8

10 9 8 7 6 5 4 3 2 1

Chronicle Books
275 Fifth Street, San Francisco, CA 94103

CONTENTS

ALL-PURPOSE EXCUSES

It looks like rain.

■

I have a bad back.

■

I'm allergic.

■

I overslept.

I'll pay you back tomorrow.

■

We gave at the office.

■

We gave at home.

The check is in the mail.

I forgot my wallet.

■

I'm out of checks.

■

I'm over my credit card limit.

I don't have anything to wear.

I didn't know it was loaded.

■

I thought you were going to call me.

■

My watch stopped.

■

I don't really wear glasses.

*This is going to hurt me
more than it hurts you.*

■

You'll thank me later.

■

Believe me, it's better this way.

The bus broke down.

My car wouldn't start.

■

The train was late.

■

The flight was cancelled.

■

I couldn't find a place to park.

My other phone is ringing.

*I think I'm coming down
with something.*

■

Someone's at the door.

■

I just followed the instructions.

■

I forgot where I parked my car.

It's too expensive.

■

It looks too cheap.

■

I meant sometime, not now.

■

*I thought you were going
to do it right away.*

The sun was in my eyes.

I have a plane to catch.

■

I have a stomachache.

■

You started it.

■

I have to do my French homework.

I couldn't hear
because the TV was on.

■

I couldn't hear
because the water was running.

■

I couldn't hear
because I had my headphones on.

My dog ate it.

It must have shrunk.

■

It was a gift.

■

It was dark when I put my socks on.

■

I didn't think anyone would notice.

I just washed my hair.

I'm expecting an important phone call.

■

I'm wearing the wrong shoes.

■

I have to get a haircut.

■

I'll write soon.

I don't have my glasses on.

■

There's no room.

■

I asked you first.

■

I was only trying to help.

I have to go home and walk the dog.

I couldn't hear what you were saying.

■

I didn't understand what you meant.

■

I knew that, but I forgot.

■

You said you would.

I never said that.

■

I don't remember saying that.

■

That's not what I meant.

■

You must have misunderstood.

Someone must have taken it.

■

I didn't think it mattered.

■

It's too crowded.

■

There's no one there.

I had one too many.

I was about to take a nap.

•

I was in the tub.

•

They never called back.

•

I didn't know you were listening.

No thanks, I'm stuffed.

I just remembered
I'm supposed to meet someone.

■

It's been so long I forgot how.

■

I have something on my contact lens.

You can borrow it
as soon as I finish using it.

■

I'll bring it right back.

■

I thought you had the keys.

The batteries must be dead.

．

The button must have been stuck.

．

The film was loaded wrong.

．

The VCR was programmed for the wrong day.

I don't have any change.

It's too hot to cook.

.

It's too cold to get out of bed.

.

I did the dishes last time.

It's too high to reach.

■

I can't bend over that far.

■

The cat's on my lap.

I thought you were joking.

I tried to call you.

.

It won't stain.

.

Winning isn't that important to me.

.

It will grow back.

The parking meter must be broken.

∎

I didn't see the NO PARKING sign.

∎

I wasn't blocking the driveway.

The light wasn't red yet.

■

I wasn't speeding.

■

I had the right-of-way.

We were just sitting down to dinner.

■

I'm saving room for dessert.

■

The lid wasn't on tight.

■

I don't want to get my hair wet.

I couldn't get a cab.

I was doing it for you.

■

I was just minding my own business.

■

I wasn't ready yet.

■

I can't talk right now.

I didn't see you coming.

We're out of gas.

My alarm didn't go off.

■

My answering machine is broken.

■

Traffic was backed up.

■

It was your idea.

It was a slip of the tongue.

I'm a vegetarian.

.

I don't believe in following recipes.

.

It's fresh frozen.

.

I have to pick up my cleaning.

EXCUSES FOR WORK

I don't have my calendar with me.

.

The fax machine was out of paper.

.

It's not on my priority list.

It was a sales and marketing decision.

■

The weather is too beautiful to go to work.

■

The weather is too awful to go to work.

I'm all tied up.

■

I'm on another line.

■

Let me get back to you on that.

The computer is down.

I just started here.

∎

That's not my job.

∎

I was on vacation.

I never got the message.

■

We have a new phone system.

■

I can't find the disk.

It's close enough for government work.

■

Let me put you on hold for just a minute.

■

You must have been cut off.

It must be a clerical error.

My hard disk crashed.

■

It wasn't my idea.

■

No one ever told me.

I'm looking into it.

.

I'm out of business cards.

.

I'm in the middle of a meeting.

EXCUSES FOR ROMANCE

I'm married.

■

You're married.

■

We're married.

I'm too old for that.

■

You're too young for that.

■

We don't know each other well enough.

Next time will be better.

.

This never happened to me before.

.

I thought you weren't coming back today.

My parents won't let me.

Not tonight, honey, I have a meeting.

■

I had to stay late at the office.

■

I didn't know you cared.

■

Nobody's perfect.

I never make plans that far in advance.

.

That was so long ago I can't remember.

.

I warned you about me.

.

You made me love you.

I have two left feet.

EXCUSES FOR CHILDREN

He's just going through a stage.

■

Her father dressed her.

■

It's time for his nap.

They never act like this at home.

■

They must have had too much sugar.

■

They kept us up all night.

I have the kids this weekend.

He's just like his father.

■

She's just like her mother.

■

He has an ear infection.